Masters of Momentum

Using Your Small Victories to Catapult
You into a Series of Opportunities

By K.W. Williams

Copyright 2017 by K.W. Williams

Published by Make Profits Easy LLC

Profitsdaily123@aol.com

facebook.com/MakeProfitsEasy

Table of Contents

Introduction 4
Chapter 1: Understanding Momentum 8
Chapter 2: Motivation and How to Build It 19
Chapter 3: Results and Rewards 27
Chapter 4: Consistency and Routine 37
Chapter 5: Learning and Teaching Patience 42
Chapter 6: Letting Go and Letting it Flow 51
Chapter 7: Knowing When to Take Charge 60
Chapter 8: Building Confidence 69
Chapter 9: What to Do when Momentum Dies 77
Chapter 10: Momentum in Your Day 85
Chapter 11: Emotional Momentum 95
Conclusion 103

Introduction

Major success may seem like the result of luck or of years of grueling hard work. While it is true that success can arise from hard work and ideal circumstances, there is a little known secret about success: momentum. Most major success arises from smaller successes. Successful people, such as entrepreneurs and investors, know how to use momentum to turn their small wins into huge ones. And you can learn how to do this too.

You don't have to burn the midnight oil, lose friends, and sacrifice quality time with your family just to be successful. You just have to learn how to use timing to your advantage. You have to learn how to recognize great opportunities and seize upon them without fear. Perhaps most importantly of all, you have to have a success-oriented mindset and try your hardest to spot ways to advance your victories into larger ones.

Within these pages, you will learn how to master the momentum of success in your life. Consider it a Domino Effect. You do something that works out well, so you let that success tumble into a greater one. You never stop working and pushing and making good decisions. You don't let stasis set in and halt your success. One success builds upon another, until success is piling up for you on its own with minimal effort on your part. This book will show you how to utilize this Domino Effect. It will show you when to exert effort and when to sit back and just let momentum work for you.

By the end of this book, you will be in a position to enjoy far more success in your life. It does not matter what you want to be successful in. Be it business, love, fitness, health, wealth, or creative ventures, you can be successful. You will know how to use momentum to your advantage and you will possess one of the most powerful secrets known to man for succeeding at anything that you try.

The beginning is often the hardest part. This is when you must put in the most work to get your first success. But once you taste victory, it's all uphill from there. Life will work with you if you let it. Most people either give up too soon or become over-involved and mess up the work that momentum does for them. You, however, are about to learn how to avoid making such mistakes. Soon, you will be successful in everything you attempt because you know how to use the universe's natural momentum to gain more and more victory.

Stop micromanaging, overworking, and giving up. Let go of the sense that you are overwhelmed. Instead, use momentum to your advantage.

Chapter 1: Understanding Momentum

So clearly this book is about momentum and using it to create a chain reaction of events that lead to big success. That sounds great, right? But what exactly is momentum? Understanding momentum is the first step in being able to create it and master it.

What Momentum Is

Momentum is a forward push. It is, in essence, a Domino Effect. But instead of this force pushing dominos down, it is building successes up to an ultimate victory. A mixture of timing, strategy, motivation, and positivity all help create the push that beings momentum. Once momentum starts, it can easily be halted by stasis and stagnation, where people get bored or unfocused and lose interest. Keeping momentum going requires some effort, but not too much.

You don't ever want to kill momentum. There are numerous things that can kill it, which I discuss in the section after next. Instead, you want to feed it. Let it grow. Let it flow and create success for you. When you are operating on momentum, you are a leader, either of yourself or of many people. Therefore, you must fuel momentum. Good leaders always work to create and maintain momentum. Only bad leaders will crush it and make a team's efforts disintegrate into chaos.

Momentum feels great. It is basically life on autopilot, with some input from you. When momentum takes over, you enjoy success after success. You feel that your work is meaningful and that you have a shot at victory. You have hope, self-esteem, and enthusiasm. The end goal grows ever closer and you just keep working toward it, never wanting to give up. Momentum makes goal achievement much easier and allows you to push yourself and your team without over exerting everyone. The work will not be overwhelming; rather, the sense of success you get from it will be.

Momentum essentially builds off of the endings of successfully completed projects or goal milestones. Once you enjoy a small success or victory, momentum allows you to build on that and roll onto the next project. It carries you like a tide into success on your next project. You have to make some effort to begin each project, but momentum will help carry you to its successful completion.

Don't Get Momentum Confused with Other Things

A lot of people start to blur the lines between momentum and things like motivation. They assume that momentum refers to giving or receiving positive feedback and encouragement, reaching successes, completing goal milestones, and even feeling excited and passionate and loving what they do. While these things are all instrumental in fueling momentum and keeping people involved in projects, they are not what momentum is.

Being positive and supportive of yourself and your team members is essential to keeping momentum going. It's key to any project. But it is not the only thing that keeps projects going. A sense of success and a drive to move forward on a project or mission is what truly constitutes momentum. You have to inspire this sense within yourself by observing your victories, wanting to press forward, and choosing to use previous victories to leapfrog into even bigger ones. If you are a team leader, you must inspire this sense within your subordinates the same way. Doing this is the only way that you can create and maintain momentum. Things like motivation, passion, and success are all things that can help you create and fuel this force within you or within your team. However, these things can exist without momentum and are not truly what momentum is.

What Kills Momentum

One of the main things that kills momentum is stasis. Stasis happens when you stop pressing forward. You spend too long in one place in life, instead of working toward new goals and finding new causes to take on. You take too long to make decisions and to perform work necessary for goal completion. The saying "out of sight, out of mind" is a very apt way to describe how stasis happens. Once you disappear from the spotlight for even a moment, people will forget about you and you may even forget about how important your success was to you in the first place. Then, you no longer matter, your project no longer matters, and no one will want to help you out and push you forward again.

Another huge killer of momentum are difficulties and roadblocks that people impose. Having to stop work to deal with an unruly team member or having to ask for permission to proceed on your project halts everything for a while. Sometimes the setback is easy to overcome, but more often than not, it's not. That's why autonomy and harmony is essential within your team so that you can continue rolling along with no hiccups.

Negativity can kill momentum because it kills the motivation that drives momentum. If you are more focused on your fears or your weaknesses than your hope and your strengths, you will hold back. This creates forces against you and prevents you from feeling free enough to continue moving along toward ultimate success.

You want to be positive and upbeat and you want to believe in yourself and whoever you are working with.

Another thing that creates major hiccups that can disrupt the flow of work and ultimately kill momentum is micromanaging. Controlling people or events too much creates a lot of extra work for you. It also distracts you from your goal. This bottlenecks your progress forward. Instead, learn to let things go that don't matter. Also learn to accept things and to not try to be perfect.

What Builds Momentum

While a number of things kill momentum, a number of things also nurture it. One of the main ways that you can nurture momentum is to break your goals down into small increments that are more manageable. That way, when you complete a goal, you receive a reward and you notice that you are making progress, even if you haven't reached your desired end result yet. So when working on a project, break it down into smaller parts. Use the successful victories from each part to catapult yourself and your team into the next step.

Encourage and practice forward thinking. You must keep your mind on your ultimate success at all times. Don't let some small inconvenience or hiccup in your plans make you stall. Instead, push through each challenge, and let your eagerness to reach the other side drive you. View each victory as a small step in the march forward and keep marching.

Momentum is the process of building off of each success that you enjoy. So when you become successful at something, don't just grin and sit back. Push forward. Make a new goal or move on to the next step as soon as you can. Stopping at any time can create the stasis that is so dangerous to momentum.

Finally, letting things flow is essential to allowing momentum to happen. You can't manage every little thing or you kill momentum. Just let success happen. Let things go that don't really matter. Avoid distractions and stay focused on the end result. Work through setbacks without despair. And don't constantly monitor how successful you are. Success will become apparent suddenly and surprisingly. Consider music artists who are not famous.

Suddenly, they are shocked when an album hits platinum and they find themselves in a new world of celebrity. There is no way to really monitor success and trying to monitor it distracts you from moving forward.

Chapter 2: Motivation and How to Build It

Motivation is the first step in creating momentum. You can't set off a chain of success if you aren't psyched up about whatever project you are trying to complete successfully. Motivation is the drive that you need to set the chain in motion. Motivating yourself and others is actually not very difficult, but it's essential for everyone to stay dedicated and interested in the tasks at hand. Sometimes, the daily grind can kill motivation and make you lose sight of why you started this mission in the first place. Renewing motivation is an essential skill to possess if you want to be successful.

Don't Get Complacent

Once you complete a goal successfully, it is a big mistake to just stop trying. Having the same goals causes you to get bored, which kills momentum and lets stasis set in. You need to keep raising the bar on your goals with each success. This keeps you motivated and eager to accomplish the next thing.

As soon as you complete one goal, congratulate yourself and anyone that you may be working with. Then set the next goal, which should be a little harder. Achieving this goal pushes you to keep working hard and bettering yourself. It is also more achievable, since you have confidence and experience from your previous success and you also know what you are capable of.

View goals as rungs on a ladder. The first few rungs may be easy to climb. The nearer you get to the top of the ladder, the harder they are to climb because they are steeper and higher than below. Nevertheless, you are now accustomed to being on the ladder and you have the top in sight, so you are determined and more than able to keep climbing. If you just stop in the middle of the ladder, you won't get anywhere. And if you give up, you'll have to descend back to the ground, also not getting anywhere.

Keep Your Eyes on the Target

Each goal you complete is ideally leading up to a final target goal. This goal could be anything – a certain goal weight, being CEO of a company, successfully opening your own muffin shop, reaching a civil relationship of forgiveness and understanding with a difficult family member. That ultimate end goal is obviously something really important that you deeply want.

One way to motivate yourself is to remind yourself of this goal. Tell yourself what you want and what you need to do to get it. Let yourself remember that even if the going is hard, the destination will make it all worth it. Reminding yourself of your end goal can give you that push you need to keep working until you reach your desired end results.

It can be helpful to really visualize your end goal for a while. Close your eyes for a minute and consider how your life will look once you reach your end goal. How will you feel? How will your friends and family feel? Won't you love how you stuck it out and accomplished something great? Imagine how you will benefit and also how proud you will be of yourself.

It can also be helpful to consider how ugly life will be if you give up. Imagine how disappointed everyone will be in you and how disappointed you will be in yourself. Consider the time and resources that you will have wasted should you quit. Usually negative thoughts don't provide much motivation, but you can really push yourself if you realize how bad things will be if you don't see your mission through to the end.

Celebrate Each Victory

The ultimate killer of motivation is a sense of purposelessness and boredom. After you work on something for a while, the mission can quickly become dull. You start to lose sight of the passion and the end results that initially pushed you to take on this mission in the first place. But you can inject some novelty into your project and motivate yourself by offering yourself rewards for each milestone that you complete on your mission.

Celebrating each victory is a great way to motivate yourself and to motivate a team. Giving yourself a reward renews the novelty of the project and provides everyone with gratification. It renews the sense that everyone involved is benefiting from this mission. So when you experience any sort of victory or complete a step in the goal, reward yourself with something that you really enjoy. You could simply have a little party with your team members, or you could treat yourself to a spa day or a round of golf. Whatever provides you with gratification will serve as a sufficient reward.

Sometimes, if your motivation is lagging or your team is losing focus and drive, you can have a celebration just to congratulate everyone involved on the great work that they have been doing. This reward will help renew interest in the project and it will instill a sense of pride in everyone involved. This is why great managers will sometimes offer pizza parties or nights out for employees for no reason except to thank everyone for their dedication and effort.

Take a Break

Sometimes, you need to take a break. When you are getting exhausted, frustrated, overwhelmed, or bored, a mental health day is a good idea. Take some time off of your project to focus on you and to revitalize yourself. Do something that you enjoy and that gives you energy.

Just be wary of taking too long of a break. Long breaks kill momentum. You can't have that. Instead, take single day to reenergize. Then you will return to work with a fresh perspective and more energy.

Chapter 3: Results and Rewards

Human beings are hardwired to want rewards for their efforts. Back in caveman days, humans would work tirelessly for food, and thus ultimately survival. Food was that ultimate reward that justified their efforts, and made them want to continue. We only do things because we want a reward in the end. The results that we aim for are really just rewards that we want to give ourselves in exchange for our hard work. When we work hard but don't see results, we tend to get restless and discouraged. We may even give up altogether. This is one of the most common reasons why diets fail, because people don't see results for a long time and they become discouraged and stop trying to eat healthier.

Sadly, instant results are very uncommon. Usually we have to work a while to see any sort of result. How do you prevent yourself, or your team members, from losing motivation and giving up when they don't see results? How can you keep reassuring everyone that results will come in time, especially if you aren't one hundred percent sure that they will?

Sometimes, you have to focus on smaller results that indicate progress. Let little results be incentives to go after bigger and better results. You can also use small rewards to help people feel that they are accomplishing something, even if the rewards are not the same as the ultimate reward that you all want from the end results of your work.

Offer Incentives

There is a reason that companies love incentive programs. Offering people incentives to keep working helps them feel that their efforts are worth it, even if they haven't yet reached their ultimate goals. If you want to create momentum and keep it going, then you need to offer yourself or others incentives. Indicate that all efforts are paying off and that progress is being made.

The easiest way to do this is to reward each small step forward or each small victory. Make a big deal about even the smallest victories. This helps pump you and everyone else up. It lets people know that they are doing the right thing and that the end goal will eventually come to completion if they keep plugging along.

People like rewards. So reward yourself or your team members with something whenever a milestone is reached or a victory is had. Have a dinner, or take a small trip somewhere. Do something rewarding and enjoyable. Dangle the promise of a reward in front of yourself and others to encourage people to move forward. For example, you can tell your team, "If you hit this number of sales by the end of the month, we'll all get a small trip to Vegas." People will want to go to Vegas so they will work hard to hit that sales number.

Let's consider this example. You are trying to lose sixty pounds. That is no small feat and you know that you are going to need months of dieting, exercising, and other lifestyle changes to lose the weight. You also know that after you lose it, you will have to keep leading a healthy lifestyle to keep the weight off. This can all be so overwhelming that you might want to quit. So break your weight loss into smaller increments. Each time you lose five pounds and hit a new target weight, use that as an incentive to show yourself that you are making progress, slowly but surely. Let your joy from losing a little bit of weight motivate you to keep pushing forward, losing more and more until you lose the full sixty pounds.

Never Discount the Small Contributions

Even the smallest steps and smallest contributions to the overall effort are worth something. Each small bit of progress made contributes to the overall mission. It brings you closer to your end goal, sometimes more quickly than you realize.

If you are leading a team of people, you should acknowledge every contribution made by every individual. Congratulate everyone on their efforts and their progress. Make it known that you notice and appreciate every little bit of work done.

If you are on this venture alone, then don't dismiss the small things that you accomplish. Yes, it is important to keep the bigger picture and the end result in mind. But it is even more important to avoid getting overwhelmed. When you make even a hint of progress, congratulate yourself and let yourself feel happy for a little bit. Don't feel disappointed and say, "This wasn't much of a step forward. I should have done better."

Don't Over Monitor Results

Results are the rewards that drive people to make progress. You want to see results. Having deadlines and quotas can help people achieve results because they see a clear time frame for goal completion which allows them to allot time and energy for a specific result. Focusing on results is motivating and drives momentum. But don't focus too much on results, or you will start to kill momentum.

Too many people obsessively monitor time, numbers, money spent, and other factors in a project. When they do this, they tend to notice how little progress is being made. They get discouraged when quotas are not met. This causes them to drop the ball on keeping momentum going.

If you don't meet a quota or goal on time, it's OK to feel a little down. But use that down feeling to push yourself to do better next time. Don't drown in despair and give up. Accept that you didn't meet your ultimate quota and push forward.

It is essential to be flexible and to let things flow when it comes to momentum. Not doing so will kill momentum. So let go of the reins a little bit. Stop being so hard on yourself and your subordinates. Say, "It's OK. But let's not do this again. Let's try harder this next time."

Create Visuals

When construction companies are working on new buildings, they often have a picture of what the completed structure will look like posted somewhere on the site. This is a great idea because it motivates people to visualize what the end result is going to be. This motivates workers and placates irritated residents who are tired of looking at construction mess. You should do the same sort of thing to give yourself a visual incentive to reach the end of your project.

Vision boards with pictures can help you actually visualize your goals. This makes them more real to you. Then you feel more inspired to reach your goals eventually. You can create a vision board and put it up in your office or bedroom, where you will always see it. Post one where your team can see it, if you are working with others on a project. Try to get pictures and quotes that show people what the completed goal will look like and to make it more real and concrete for everyone.

You can also ask people to visualize the completed project. Have everyone close their eyes and think about what the project will look like when finished and how great you will all feel knowing that you stuck out this difficult work all of the way to the end.

Chapter 4: Consistency and Routine

Consistency and routine allow for a rhythm to form in your work. This rhythm makes it easy to achieve the best results. Your project essentially becomes a well-oiled machine that runs itself. Your team and you will know exactly what to do and if you adhere to a routine that you can all agree on. As a leader, you should set this routine in place and make sure that your team adheres to it.

Daily Goals and Task Lists

Each day is a new chance to do better than the day previously. Therefore, you should start each day fresh with a new task list. This task list should clearly outline what needs to be accomplished in the course of the day. It should tie in with your task list for your entire project.

Having a daily goal makes goals more reachable for team members. Everyone will enjoy working on something new each day instead of getting bored. It also gives a purpose to each day, which prevents stasis and boredom.

Consistent Times

You want to be consistent in your organization, work, and timeframes. Consistency helps you and your team know what to expect. That way, you can all be prepared for what work needs to be done and you won't have confusion slowing down your momentum.

Have set meeting times, every day or every week, when you touch on each other's progress and review your goals. Have a set work day and set times when people are supposed to perform certain tasks.

Also be consistent with your praise and your rewards. You want to present rewards in a consistent manner with what you promise. You don't want to start promising people things and then not delivering. Prove that you are a leader of your word by being consistent and doing what you say you will do.

Don't bog your team down with a restrictive schedule that does not allow for flexibility. Life throws a lot of curve balls. Sometimes you will need to change your routine to allow for unexpected changes and turns of events. Allow this to happen. Don't fight it. Flexibility is key in adapting to life and overcoming challenges, especially unforeseen ones. Also, variety is sometimes necessary to prevent boredom, so change things up now and then. Offer new activities or a casual shirt day. Just do something that helps break up the monotony and make working on the goal fun for everyone involved.

Clear Deadlines and Timeframes

Giving everyone deadlines helps create a timeframe in which people can complete their goals. Knowing what you must do and how long you have to do it helps you get organized. When you set up a project, create milestones with deadlines.

You don't have to be overly strict with these deadlines. Don't freak out if you don't meet a specific deadline on time. It's OK. But it does mean that you have to work harder to catch up on your progress. Use this as a motivator to meet deadlines. Deadlines aren't a joke, but you don't need to stress about them so much that you kill momentum.

If you are using incentives to inspire your team, then have a clear reward schedule. Rewards should be given out after the milestone is finally met. You can offer extra incentives for people who finish their work early or on time, too.

Chapter 5: Learning and Teaching Patience

Results don't just appear overnight. Patience is key to not just giving up on a project because it doesn't yield the results you want right away. Impatience can cause you to lose hope and give up before you even have a chance.

Therefore, it's key to learn how to become patient. As a team leader, you should also teach others how to be patient. Encouraging patience within yourself and your team will help all of you maintain hope that the project can be completed in a timely manner.

Lead Breathing Exercises

When impatience reaches an uncomfortable fever pitch, it doesn't do anyone any good. You just feel miserable and you want the feeling to go away. This can make you want to quit the project. So when you feel this way, it's best for everyone if you end the feeling. It's time to step back from your work and practice calming breaths. Just close your eyes and inhale through your nose. When you exhale through your mouth, imagine all of your stress and impatience leaving your body in a great wave.

You can also lead your team on a group breathing exercise if impatience is bugging everyone. Tell everyone to breathe together for a few minutes. Perhaps play a guided meditation to help everyone relax together. Not only will everyone benefit from relaxation, but the group relaxation exercises can be a great group bonding experience that brings everyone closer and helps everyone learn how to work together supportively.

Manage Your Emotions

Emotions are powerful and run as an undercurrent to everything that we do. But when emotions run on high, they tend to distract people from work and make the workplace become unprofessional. It is essential for everyone to learn how to manage their emotions.

Find a healthy coping mechanism for people to use when their emotions start running on high. Stress balls, a punching bag, or working out all great ways to relieve stress and lower the fire of emotions.

You can also facilitate meetings when emotions start running on high. Encourage everyone to drop everything and sit in a circle. Have each person state how he or she is feeling. Then have each person come up with a viable solution for calming and healing negative emotions. If you are on a solo mission, you can use a journal to jot down and understand your emotions and find solutions.

When people are expressing anger or other negative emotions, try to frame their emotions more positively. This will inspire them to feel better. For instance, if someone is complaining about working late, say, "Well, if you work late, you will get a lot of attention from the boss. That could turn into a promotion. This could end up being a good thing!"

Remember the End Goal

Remember what you are working toward. This refreshes your will to plug on. It can also calm your impatience as it helps you recall the steps that you absolutely must make before you can reach your end goal. Remind everyone about how worthwhile the end goal is. Suggest that people use their impatience as motivation to push forward and reach the end goal more quickly.

You can all have a conversation where you share how much you want the end goal. You can talk about what you envision the end goal looking and feeling like. Everyone can feel more interested in goal completion when they spend some time talking and visualizing. You can renew your team bonds, and thus distract yourselves from your impatience. In addition, you build team spirit through this activity.

Enjoy the Moment

Sometimes focusing only on the end goal will kill your patience and trigger your impatience. You are too intent on the future that you can't handle how slowly it is coming. You should sometimes take your focus off of the end goal. Focus on the present instead. Enjoy the scenery of the present moment and the present world around you.

It can be helpful to practice mindfulness for a moment. Take just a little bit of time out of your day to count your breaths to calm your mind and restore focus on the present moment. Then take in the sensations of the world around you. Observe the ceiling and wall patterns, the smell of the air, and the weather outside. Feel each part of your body. Build awareness of the present moment. When you begin thinking of the future, draw your thoughts gently back to the present.

The end result is a huge mile marker that you can't wait to reach. But often the journey to the destination contains lots of enjoyable and important moments as well. Being able to enjoy the journey, instead of hating the journey and lusting for the destination, will make you more content with your work and your current progress.

Listen Better

Listen to yourself. When impatience flares up, don't suppress it. Instead, take some time to confront the problem. Figure out why you are impatient. Spend some time trying to figure out what drives this impatience and how to calm it down. Remember to tell yourself to let go of stress and impatience. Tell yourself how important it is to be calm and patient. The restlessness you feel won't be pleasant, so remind yourself how much better serenity feels. If you need to do yoga or meditation, then go for it.

It also important to listen to your team. Listen to their complaints and their impatience. Don't just dismiss how they feel. Be empathetic and really try to understand what they are feeling. This is the only way that you can determine a way to be kind and compassionate, in order to soothe everyone.

Find out what is making the team restless. Are they discouraged by a lack of results? Is a major deadline impending, and no one seems to be near completing it? Is one or two of the team members not quite pulling their weight, hence slowing the whole team down and frustrating those who are working hard? Once you find the source of the problem, you can figure out what to do about it.

Chapter 6: Letting Go and Letting it Flow

Many times I have mentioned letting momentum do the work for you. It is very important to not become too involved in the process. You don't want to stifle and kill momentum by becoming over-involved. You need to learn when to let go of things and just let work flow without disruption and without interruption. This is the only way that you can let momentum flow and carry you from one successful ending to another.

Letting go can be incredibly difficult for some people. Some people like to have control. They worry that things will fall apart if they step back and let life run its course. However, being able to let go is a critical skill to possess, especially when you start to become a master of momentum. Momentum will work for you, so let it. Propel yourself from the end of each victory or success to the next. Don't hold everyone up in the process by nitpicking little things that don't matter or micromanaging the team's efforts or worrying about things that don't really matter in the long run.

Relaxing and being patient are essential traits of any momentum master. You want to be able to take a deep breath and let go of worries. You need to patiently let things work themselves out. You need to be bold and confident, and understand that most things work out just fine in the end. Also have some humility and understand that you will not be able to control or fix every little thing. You are more likely to make a mess of things if you interfere too much.

Ask Yourself If It Matters

If you think that you need to change something or micromanage something, ask yourself, "How badly does this matter?" Let's say your team's ultimate goal is to create a new network for your company. But you are obsessing about the placement of buttons on the front end. Does this really matter? Or is it something small that you can let go of? If it doesn't truly lead to the successful completion of the goal, don't waste time and hold up progress by tweaking it.

It is even more complicated to manage people. If someone is doing something that you want to address or fix, ask yourself if this person's work is really that bad. Will his or her efforts ultimately hurt the team? Will they matter in six months, a year, five years? If not, then let it go and don't say anything. Micromanaging and bothering your team with small things really kills momentum and discourages team members. It is better to let people do their own thing as long as it goes toward the ultimate goal and doesn't hurt anyone.

Question if something that happens is really wrong. If it isn't, then move on. If it is, then exert as little effort as possible to make sure that it is corrected.

Pick Your Battles

Especially when you are working with other people, you really need to learn how to pick your battles. There are things that you can easily ignore and things that need to be addressed. The interactions that you have with your team members should be smooth and pleasant. Even if you lose your tempers with each other, as long as you can both get over it and keep working, you are golden.

Let go of minor spats or temper flares. There is no need to hold a grudge or keep harping on a small disagreement. What you shouldn't let go of is unprofessional, demeaning, or harassing behavior. So decide how severe the issue is before you decide to make a big deal out of it. Usually, it is best to simply move on. Alternatively, you can settle things with your team members in private without making it a huge deal at work.

If a co-worker is rude, decide if you can get over it or not. You can make a big deal out of it if this rude treatment prevents you from working well together. However, it takes a lot of effort to correct co-workers and people rarely change. You can save a lot of emotional energy and effort if you choose to simply ignore rude behavior that doesn't really tear down your ability to get your job done right.

If a co-worker has an annoying little habit, do you really need to create a big ruckus and start a fight over it? Can you ignore the little quirks and flaws that your team members have? Can you overlook little mistakes? If so, then do so. You don't want to become the leader who picks everyone apart and demands everyone to adhere to your ideas of what is right or wrong. Only get involved when someone's actions are detrimental to the success of the mission.

Don't Fix What Isn't Broken

It is time to decide if things are really broken and need to be fixed or if you are just nitpicking. Look at how important a problem is. Does it hurt the overall functioning of the team? Does it serve some sort of destructive force on the overall goal? Is it causing disruption in the work flow? Does it tear down your goals or inhibit your progress?

Just because something bothers you doesn't always mean that it is a big problem. Get input from others about how bad something is.

Decide with other people if it can be worked with or if you need to put in some effort to change it.

If something isn't actually a disruptive problem, then it works well enough. You can address it later if need be. But you need to dedicate your time, resources, and energy toward your goal completion. Don't waste time on fixing things that aren't broken. Doing so will only cause more damage than good.

Stop Checking on Progress

Stop constantly checking your progress to see where you or your team is at on the journey toward your ultimate goal destination. Just trust that you are making progress. Focus more on working than on measuring results and progress. Ultimately, momentum tends to sneak up on you and surprise you with success, so trust in momentum. You will only hold up the team if you keep monitoring progress too much. Getting a good idea of where the team is at is not a bad idea, just to make sure that you are all on track, but it's not healthy to focus on measuring progress too much.

Chapter 7: Knowing When to Take Charge

It is essential to know when to lean back and let things run on autopilot. But momentum doesn't run on its own. It needs your effort to keep it going. You must keep moving forward. That's why it is equally essential to know when to take charge and take action on a project. You can't leave everything up to other people, to Fate, or to momentum, or things will fall apart and momentum will die.

But how can you tell when you need to take charge? Sometimes, you will just know. You see that action is needed and that your project will fail if you don't take that action. Other times, it may not be so clear. Here are some times when you need to take action immediately. Don't wait around when you recognize any of these signs.

The Team is Losing Focus

The minute that the team starts to lose focus, disaster is headed its way. You must intervene. Be the heroic astronaut who prevents an asteroid from hitting the Earth by intervening and returning the team to what they should be focused on.

You will know that your team is losing focus when they start to goof around and procrastinate on work. They may talk about other projects or side projects more than the main project. They may start to brainstorm ideas for new ventures that have nothing to do with the current project. Certain team members may stop showing up to work consistently and may seem bored when they're there.

You will know that you are losing focus when you start to daydream or want to do other things. If you no longer think much about your end goal, you are losing focus.

Draw everyone's attention back to the end goal. Emphasize how important it is. Let people know that they can pursue other projects when this one is completed.

The Team is Unmotivated or Discouraged

When people start to complain that they are not getting anywhere, you can be sure that your team is losing motivation and getting discouraged. This means that the team is rapidly losing steam. Not wanting to get to work and not wanting to get out of bed in the morning is another worrisome sign.

You can renew the team's motivation with a pep talk. Remind everyone why they started in the first place. Remind them to be patient and that millionaires are rarely made overnight. Point out what progress you have made and make a big deal about even the smallest steps that you guys have made in the right direction.

Also start offering motivating incentives. Alternatively, scare your team by telling them how badly it will turn out should they quit now.

A Challenge Arises

Something comes up that disrupts the flow of work. You can't just sit back and expect things to work themselves out. You have to get your hands dirty. Immediately recognize the problem and address it with your team. Then all of you need to brainstorm solutions. Think of alternatives to your current plan or solutions to the challenge that will work for the majority. Help people make wise decisions toward a satisfying solution. Make it clear what each team member can do to help overcome the challenge. Use the challenge as motivation to bond the team and press forward with ever more determination.

Team Members Are Disagreeing with Each Other

Teams must work together in harmony and unison. When team members start having problems getting along, you need to get involved, before they disrupt the entire project for everybody. You need to ask the team members to take some time away from each other. Then sit them down and facilitate a mature discussion about what is bothering them. Propose solutions and watch them talk it out. Make them stop when they start raising voices or getting nowhere.

If the entire team seems to be splintering at the seams, maybe it's time for some team building exercises. Have a friendly basketball game or night out on the town. Play a word game. These exercises can facilitate a feeling of unity and cohesion again that can transfer over into work.

You Feel Overwhelmed

When you or anyone begins to feel overwhelmed, you are overexerting yourself. You must take action to stop the feeling or you're heading into the danger zone of wanting to give up. Being overwhelmed is never good.

Maybe you should go for a walk in the park. Take a mental health day. Propose that your team all takes a yoga class or lead people with some yoga moves at the office. The purpose is to help everyone soothe their stress. It also enables everyone to step back from the project and gain a fresh perspective about how to go about achieving the next milestone.

Working yourself to death and working your team to death does not do your project any favors. Being overwhelmed is a bad sign that you are getting into a mire of stress and exhaustion.

You need to take care of this feeling right away to prevent it from corroding your team's will to press on.

You Begin to Question Yourself

Doubts start out small and blossom into huge fears that can cripple you or your team. When you start to question why you are doing something in the first place, or if this is what you really want, or if you are doing the right thing, then you are heading into a dangerous place.

It is best to talk about your doubts openly or write them in a journal. Have everyone on your team do this. Then work on reminding each other why you started this in the first place. Try to reaffirm the reasons you are doing this project. Remember how completion will benefit all of you or the cause that you are working for.

Chapter 8: Building Confidence

Confidence plays a huge role in momentum. If you are insecure and doubtful, you will hold yourself back and prevent momentum from carrying along on its current. But if you are surer of yourself, you won't have such issues. Building confidence in yourself and in your team is essential for momentum to work. You want to be sure of yourself and to never hang back. You want to be bursting with pride and enthusiasm, energy that attracts success. And you want to believe in yourself and your chances of success, or you won't try hard and you won't create the forward push that triggers momentum.

Value Everyone's Hard Work

Everyone on the team is valuable. Everyone contributes something toward the end result that you all want. Therefore, you must make sure that everyone feels valued. You must take some time to praise and reward each person for their efforts.

It is especially flattering when you recognize individuals for their achievements. If someone does great work one day, congratulate him or her in front of everyone else. But be sure to tell the whole team that they were all exceptional. Give out thank you cards if you want to be more discreet.

It is also essential to thank your team for their hard work each day. Be gracious and make your team members want to come back to work the next day. Have an end-of-day meeting where you tell everyone how wonderfully they performed that day. Thank them each individually as they leave the room.

Try to remember specific details about each individual on their team. Ask them how their father is doing or how is their new baby. People love feeling like you pay attention and listen to them. They like individually tailored attention. Also jot down birthdays on a calendar and host birthday parties or give out cards.

Pretend to Be Confident, Even if You Aren't

Confidence is represented by a series of postures and behaviors. But it can be emulated and built from these postures and behaviors, as well. Appearing to have confidence makes others believe in you. As a result, you start to gain confidence in reality. You basically need to fake it until you make it.

As the representative and leader of your team, you need to have the most confidence of all. You need to believe in what you're doing. Sometimes, though, you have no idea what you're doing. How can you get people to respect you and follow you if you don't believe in what you're doing? Well, you just have to pretend like you are sure of yourself. Others will observe your behavior and follow suit. Your team will feel confident if their leader is confident.

It's not easy to pretend to know what you are doing if you have no clue. But you can instill confidence in your team and eventually in yourself by holding your head high and your spine straight with your shoulders thrown back. Walk with purpose. Give firm handshakes. When you talk to people, don't waver or stutter, but instead hold eye contact and pretend to know exactly what you are talking about. Use fancy language to make it seem like you are articulate and know your subject matter in depth.

Get Educated

If you don't know what you're doing or if you don't have any certainty that your project will work as you hope, then you can really boost your confidence by educating yourself more. Finding out more about your subject matter and gaining a stronger understanding of the industry that you are working in will both increase your chances of success. They will consequently boost your confidence. You won't be as lost or as scared once you have details and a solid grasp of the whole picture.

There is no shame in asking others for input. You can ask your team members, or other workers in your company, or other entrepreneurs. Find people who have been through what you are going through. Now the Internet also has a wealth of supportive forums and articles that you can check out for goal completion and momentum advice. These things can all really help get more educated and figure out a foolproof plan for success. Don't let fear make you give up; let it drive you to figure out a way.

Be Specific

One surefire way to kill a team's confidence is to be vague about what the team is meant to be. As team members get confused, they stop putting in their hard work. They become trepid and uncertain. As a leader, you need to be specific and clear.

It's OK to ask people if they understand you. You can even ask them to explain what you said back to you to prove that they understand you. Possibly write this or create graphs or Power Points to drive your point home. Hand out little instructional guides or pamphlets detailing the day's work. These activities may seem redundant, but it's better than having a misinformed or confused team. Sometimes team members may be too embarrassed to speak up and ask for clarification if they are confused, so spare them that trouble by double checking that they understand you.

Also be specific with your own personal goals. Have a very clear outline of what you want to accomplish in your mind. Write it down if you have to. You won't feel confident and you won't make progress if you have only a vague idea of what you're doing next.

Make sure to also have clear steps for goal completion. Breaking things down into smaller, bite-sized steps usually helps people feel more confident that they are capable of finishing the overall goal. If you need to make it easier on yourself or others by changing a goal, then do so. You would rather invite success than failure and defeat.

Chapter 9: What to Do when Momentum Dies

Ideally, momentum on your project will never be killed. Think of momentum as a train. It takes a lot of energy to get a train rolling. Once it starts, though, it gains rhythm, power, and speed, until it becomes deadly and hard to stop. If the conductor ever has to pull the brakes, though, the train comes to a screeching halt and it takes a ton of energy to get it going again. Breaking the flow of momentum is a bad thing because it creates a lot of trouble in the long run. You have to expend a lot of energy on getting momentum up and moving again, and that's energy that you could have instead spent rolling on toward success and victory.

But should momentum ever die on a project, it's not the end of the world. It is possible to save momentum and build it up again. Should you ever lose momentum, try building it back up again with these tips.

Don't Wait Any Longer

The minute momentum dies, it becomes an emergency situation that must be dealt with promptly. If you wait any longer, you may lose any chance at all of regaining momentum. So focus on building momentum back up immediately. You don't have much time to lose.

The more urgency with which you react to this situation, the more likely you can salvage momentum. You will sense that you need to get back to work. Your team will feel the urgency as well. Everyone will become more inspired to get back on track.

You should also emphasize to yourself and others how important momentum is. Tell everyone "We can't lose momentum!" Let them know how crucial it is that you all start work again immediately. Sometimes, urgency is what people need to give them a good push.

Increase the sense of urgency by cracking down on deadlines. Demand a little more effort this time around to reach goal completion by a certain time. Often, people will be willing to work harder for a short spurt in order to catch up.

You can also use competitiveness to your advantage. Look at other people or teams who still have momentum. You want to be like them, right? So create a little competition that makes you and your team want to double their effort to catch up to others who are now ahead.

Remind Everyone why They Started

If momentum is gone, then people are probably unmotivated about the project. It is time to remind everyone why they started in the first place. You need to tell yourself or your team how important the goal completion is. Remind them to visualize the end result again. This can inspire everyone to feel the same passion that they did when they originally started.

Sometimes a guilt trip will work in this case. "Don't you remember why we started this whole thing? Don't you care anymore?" Make people feel guilty for not caring anymore. This can inspire people to remember their values and goals and want to work hard for them again.

Give Pep Talks

You are the coach leading a team to victory. You must act accordingly. This means that you need to be positive, inspiring, and motivational. You have to give pep talks. It's time to say what needs to be said to lead people to victory.

Watch some pep talks that coaches give their teams before big games. Notice how much energy and enthusiasm these coaches exude. They seem quite urgent, but also quite convinced that their team can win. They tell the team to focus on that trophy and to really want that trophy. They may also tell their team how horrible losing will be. Then they psyched everyone up with a team cheer.

Adopt their energy and their philosophy. Focus on gains and tell your team the positives that will happen if they commit to the goal again. You can also bring up the negative and show them what they have to lose if they don't work hard.

Let's look at an example. You are trying to quit smoking. Your plan is to reduce the number of cigarettes that you smoke each day and to eventually just smoke an e-cigarette with lower and lower percentages of nicotine fluid. By the end of the year you plan to be nicotine-free. But then a stressful event occurs and you start smoking more than usual. You lose momentum and now you fear that you will never be able to quit smoking. Look at yourself in the mirror and tell yourself, "Do you know what will happen to you if you quit? You will get very sick! But if you stick with this, think of how much better you'll feel. Think of how much money you'll save. At the end of the year, you will be able to afford the down payment on a new car!"

Find New Incentives

If momentum is lost, then clearly what you have been doing is no longer working. The rewards that you previously offered are no longer good enough to get people going. So it's time to think up some new incentives to motivate everyone to keep working hard and to believe in the possibility of results.

As I said before, competition is a great incentive that you can use if your team is lagging. People love to win. If you make work a fun game where people must beat another team, then people will be more likely to engage and work hard. You can even divide up your team into smaller teams and have them compete with each other.

You should also offer people something big that will wow them. A big trip, a big bonus, a big promotion. Promise people a bigger reward than what you originally promised. People will develop renewed passion to get this bigger and better reward.

Chapter 10: Momentum in Your Day

Thus far, I have talked about using momentum to complete goals involving work or making major life changes. The focus of this book has primarily been on completing huge goals using momentum to build off of smaller successes. But what if you don't have a big goal? What if you just want the momentum to complete your regular daily tasks and have energy to attack your to-do list with vigor?

You're not silly if you have simpler goals. Many people have trouble getting out of bed in the morning and getting everything done in the course of the day. They may feel hopeless or bored and they may not want to do things that they need to do. Life can be stressful and even boring, killing your motivation and throttling your joy. Momentum can be extremely helpful in just getting through your day-to-day life. It can be especially helpful if you struggle with depression or are in a stressful situation, such as being a new parent. It can also help you if you are recovering from some sort of trauma, illness, injury, or major setback and need help moving forward and rebuilding your life.

That is why you need to build momentum throughout your day. This momentum will make it easier to do the tasks that you need to do. It will help you push forward and complete your basic day-to-day goals.

Have a To-Do List and Goals

Every night, decide what you want to accomplish the following day. Throw in your normal daily activities, such as house chores or going to work, but also add something that you have been putting off, such as rearranging the pantry or staining the fence in your yard. Then organize this to-do list according to priorities, and allot time frames in which you must complete each task. The most important things should be done first in the day. Then you can get to less important things later.

Then, throughout the day, follow your to-do list strictly. Put off things like Facebook, TV, and other unimportant activities until you have completed your most important tasks. Only allow leisure when you have completed everything on the list. Each task that you complete, check off. The sensation of completion that you get from crossing items off of your list will build the momentum that helps carry you into completing your next task. You will love completing your whole to-do list and getting around to things that you have been putting off.

Find a Reason to Do Something

If you are lacking motivation, find ways to motivate yourself. Having a clear purpose and finding meaning in the tasks that you do will motivate you. For instance, no one likes doing dishes. But you can motivate yourself by reminding yourself, "If I don't do the dishes, they'll pile up and stink. That will attract flies and ants. The food will harden on the plates and make my job a lot harder later." Psyche yourself up by reminding yourself why you must do each task on your to-do list. Imagine how nice it will be after you finally complete the task. Remember, motivation is the key to creating and fueling momentum, so add some motivation to your daily life.

Challenge Yourself

Doing something challenging and exerting each day helps create momentum. You can start each day with a vigorous exercise routine or engage in a mind-bending puzzle. Completing the challenge will psyche you up to complete the rest of the tasks in your to-do list. It will also make other tasks seem easier, so that you won't have as much of a problem completing them.

It is also very motivating to have something interesting that adds a bit of spark to your day. You don't want to be bored or you won't gain momentum. Give yourself something stimulating that you look forward to each day.

Vary Your Routine but Be Consistent

Routine is important for momentum. But you don't want to get so bogged down by routine that you get bored and stop feeling motivated. You also don't want to prevent the flow of momentum from carrying you from one task to another by adhering to a rigid routine too strictly.

Have a regular bed time, rise time, and meal times. Have a fairly regular time to do chores and to work out. You will get used to your routine and you will want to stick to it. This will motivate you to keep doing certain things that you must do every day.

But look for ways to spice things up to prevent boredom. Go out and try a new activity every weekend. Take a different route home from the grocery store. Watch different shows on TV and check out new books or movies.

Change Your Lifestyle

It is important to lead a lifestyle that gives you energy and doesn't bog you down with guilt. You can start by cutting out habits that kill your motivation, such as sleeping in late or eating food that makes you want to sleep. Look at your lifestyle and determine where you could use some changes. Then make those changes. You will feel better and you will gain momentum as you successfully implement and follow these lifestyle changes.

One great place to start is to eat a big, healthy breakfast with lots of fruit sugar and protein. This breakfast will start your day out right. You can also try getting sufficient sleep and cutting out nighttime activities that make you lose sleep. Waking up early is the hallmark habit of most successful people, so work on setting your alarm earlier and earlier. A strenuous activity, such as jogging or attending a workout class, can give you drive and energy to finish out your day as well.

Reward Yourself

You need to reward yourself for everything that you do. Rewards motivate people and provide positive reinforcement. They can train you to want to complete tasks for the reward that you get in the end. Find rewards that matter to you and don't feel ashamed to reward yourself.

For instance, if you adhere to your diet and eat clean all week, go ahead and reward yourself on Saturday with a slice of chocolate cake. When you finally finish a remodeling project that you have been putting off for months, crack open a cold one or pour yourself a glass of wine and go out with friends that night. When you have finally reached your savings goal, buy yourself something small but nice. Treat yourself now and then and feel proud of yourself. Not everyone can overcome procrastination and lack of motivation but you did, so pat yourself on the back.

Chapter 11: Emotional Momentum

Emotional momentum is using positive emotions to inspire other positive emotions and bring about change in your emotional state. You can use the concept of momentum to keep building on top of one positive thought or emotion until you are finally in a happy and content state.

This type of momentum can really help you if you are feeling down and need to life your mood up. It can also help you become stronger in character and more proactive. It can help you build up confidence and repair your relationships or approach new people that you are interested in. If you suffer from depression, it can help you develop positive thinking habits to lift you out of your rut of despair and negativity.

Trigger Happy Thoughts

Thoughts in themselves create a sort of momentum. This momentum can be positive or negative. The more positive thoughts that you think, the more positive emotional momentum you will create for yourself.

Start with positive affirmations in the morning. Tell yourself some positive things about yourself and about life. Ask yourself, "How can I make this day amazing?" You are getting the ball rolling and inviting more positive thinking into your mind when you do this. Don't ever begin the day with negativity or you create negative emotional momentum that will tear your mood down for the rest of the day.

Also keep a gratitude journal and write down three things that you are grateful for each day. This will start a momentum where you think about how much you really have and how blessed you are. When things get tough, read through this journal or reflect on the good things in your life. Replace criticizing yourself with positive thoughts about your good qualities and traits. You will become more grateful and hence you will feel better.

When you think a negative thought, chase it with a positive thought. Then keep thinking positively. For instance, if you're facing a hurdle in life and you start to think "I can't handle this," chase that thought away by thinking, "I can find a solution to this." Follow that thought up with more positive thoughts about what you can do to help yourself through this challenging situation and how great your life is regardless of the problems that you have.

Stress Relief

When stressful events occur, you can easily lose momentum and balance. But balance is essential to momentum. When you become overstressed, it's best not to freak out or numb out. Doing either of those things will cause momentum to stop and you will start to think negatively again.

Instead, ask yourself, "Is this worth being stressed over? Will this even matter in a year? In six months?" Questioning your stress can help you learn to let go of it. Then you start to learn not to become stressed about little things all of the time. You create a calm momentum that carries you through things that would normally stress you out in the future.

It's best to step back when you become stressed. Do some yoga, drink relaxing tea, take a hot shower, or visit a spa. Do anything that calms you down. Then return to your day-to-day and find proactive solutions to whatever is causing you stress. Don't over think and don't keep picking away at your problems, or you will only double your stress.

When you refuse to let stress get to you, and instead keep pushing forward, you create a sort of momentum of calm. Stress stops bothering you as much. The stress coping skills you adopt will build upon one another, helping you overcome stress even more completely in the future.

Conservational Momentum

Not knowing what to say to someone can make you feel embarrassed and awkward. It's easy to get over that feeling by using conversational momentum. Essentially listen very well to the other person. Then build future conversations based on things you talked about in the past. For instance, if someone mentions that they hate mustard, you can come back at another time and say, "I remember how you say you hate mustard. I read this article about how mustard is actually good for you and it made me think of you." This is just one example of the many ways that you can use a previous conversation to catapult you into future conversations. Good-bye awkwardness!

Relationship Momentum

Don't let your insecurities get in the way of great relationships. You can use momentum to essentially ease into a relationship. You can do this by having positive thoughts about the relationship and by never letting things drop between you two. From day one, try to move forward with the relationship by continuing to build on conversations and get to know each other. Call or text every day and go out on regular dates or make friendly dates. When you have problems, don't think about giving up, but rather move forward toward solutions. Don't dwell on the past, but rather let the past form a foundation for your future together. Build upon the past and learn from your mistakes with each other to create more success as you go on in your relationship. Celebrate milestones, such as anniversaries, to remind each other how far you have come and all that you have experienced together. That success can catapult you into continued success further down the road.

Conclusion

Now you have learned the little-known secret to success. You have learned how to use the universe's natural momentum to essentially roll out a small victory into a larger one. You know how to put in work and use timing until the universe is essentially doing the work for you. All it takes is a little shove, and you can start a massive chain of positive events.

You should not do anything to obstruct this positive flow of energy and success. Instead, you must learn patience and you must learn to let go sometimes. Nevertheless, momentum requires energy and work to keep it going. You must be willing to put in effort. Use things like timing, consistency, motivation, and incentives to get your team or yourself to keep moving forward. And never stall or give up. Momentum is built off of forward motion and forward thinking.

Once you learn how to master momentum, you can let it take over and put your success on autopilot. Create the first success and springboard off of it into the next one. Keep being successful until you reach your goal. You can achieve success much more easily this way. You don't have to overwork or micromanage to enjoy great success with the help of momentum.

This does not mean that momentum takes all of the work out of your success. You have to put work in. But perhaps you don't need to work as hard. Instead focus on marching forward and making progress. Don't let the momentum die.

Use motivation techniques and patience to ensure your success and to fuel momentum.

Momentum isn't just for business. You can use it for your daily life or personal goals. You can use it for relationships. You can even use it to adjust your attitude and thinking to be more positive. All kinds of changes can be brought about in your life if you employ the use of momentum to your favor. Momentum makes change easy and it makes you feel inspired to do your best.

If you are stagnant, you can revive momentum to start doing its work on your life again. Make momentum a positive thing and use it as a vehicle to draw you out of your rut. Remember that stasis is the enemy of both momentum and success. You never want to stop your progress or take too long of a break from your work.

This book has all of the secrets to mastering momentum and catapulting yourself into total victory. Don't give up on success. Instead, use momentum to bring you there. Let momentum carry you to your ultimate success.

You really can excel and achieve awesome success. You are more than capable of it. The only thing stopping you is you. So set aside your impatience and your fears, and just start building upon each success that you enjoy. You can achieve more than you ever thought possible before. Start using momentum and watch your life transform. Be prepared to be wowed!

Other books available by K.W. Williams on Kindle, paperback and audio

Lifting The Clouds: How To Support A Loved One With Depression

Meditation 101: Beat the Stress with the Power of Your Mind

The Science of Self Massage: Independently Relieve Stress Using Techniques That Target Trigger Points

Personality Decoder: Identifying and Maneuvering Around Different Personality Styles

You're Not Crazy, You're a Parent! How to Manage your Stress, Your Family and Your Work by Establishing Boundaries and Creating a Balance

Mastermind Psychology 101: How to Read Anyone and Figure out Their Motives

Loyal Friends and Real Connections: Creating True Friendships in a World of Fakers

Finding Your God: Exploring Your Spiritual Life in a Fast Paced World

Happy Is Not Enough: Finding Meaning, Purpose, and Fulfillment in Life

Own Your Life: Strategies, Tips, and Hacks to Kick Ass, Take Names, and Be at the Top of Your Game

www.ingramcontent.com/pod-product-compliance
Lightning Source LLC
Chambersburg PA
CBHW030853180526
45163CB00004B/1558